D1263467

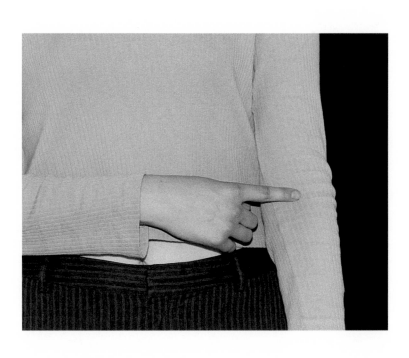

STABLE
VICES

JOANNA
PIOTROWSKA

1   Jean-François Lyotard. 'Speech Snap-
    shot'. *The Inhuman. Reflections on Time*,
    1991, English translation by G. Bennington
    and R. Bowlby, Polity Press, Cambridge,
    1988, pp. 130-1.
2   René Magritte quoted in *René Mag-
    ritte. Catalogue raisonné. Oil Paintings,
    1916-1930*, vol. I, edited by David Sylves-
    ter, Menil Foundation, Houston/Electa,
    Milan, 1992, cat. 225.
3   Ibid.
4   Ibid.

DEFENCELESS DAWN
SARA DE CHIARA

That's it, it's a problem of communication, i.e. translation. No doubt they do have a soul, but of a type different from ours, speak a language, but a bodily language (even their words are like things), they hear someone, but not us. We have to establish what they want. We record them every which way, like extraterrestrial beings. We describe their gesticulations exactly. And, you'll see, we shall decipher their idiom, they'll end up by talking to us. They will want to know, like we do. They will enter our community. There will be no more hysterics.[1]

The original title René Magritte gave to his 1928 painting which is known today as *Les jours gigantesques* (The Titanic Days) was *L'aube désarmée* (Defenceless Dawn): it was inscribed on the back of the canvas and later deleted in favour of the definitive title. *Defenceless Dawn* was suggested by Paul Nougé, the Belgian surrealist poet. Magritte had written to him, saying he was dissatisfied with his initial idea for the title, *La peur de l'amour* (Fear of Love). In the letter the artist, referring to the painting, pointed out: 'The violence is not simply external here.'[2]

This assertion may be related to what Magritte wrote in another letter sent to Marcel Lecomte, explaining that the peculiarity of this work was to be found in the way he treated the subject 'by means of a subterfuge, a reversal of the laws of space.'[3] In the canvas, which represents an attempted rape, 'the man seizes the woman; he is in the foreground; necessarily therefore the man

conceals part of the woman, the part where he is in front of her, between her and our vision. But the discovery lies in the fact that the man does not overlap the outline of the woman.'[4]

In those years Magritte was taking his first steps towards a pictorial subversion of reality, and the collision of realism and artifice here is manifested in the disturbing struggle between the two figures: a nude woman, the full volume of her fleshy body — reminiscent of the sculptural plasticity of Picasso's bathers — and the partial, flat silhouette of a clothed man.

The representation of violence, the sexual assault, is condensed in this painting almost exclusively in the figure of the woman, who is gripped by terror, as her tense lips and disjointed pose in the unequivocal gesture of rejection reveal. It seems she is stripping off the physical presence of the man, who disappears almost completely. He does not exist outside the profile of the woman's silvery body as if illuminated by the moonlight, on which the man's back is projected, like the shadow of a partial eclipse.

In Joanna Piotrowska's black and white series of photographs *Untitled*, inspired by self-defence manuals, the man, the male figure, has undergone a total eclipse. Each picture shows a young woman caught in an unnatural pose, with unbalanced postures, exaggerated twists, her hands contorted and her face often hidden by hair or fingers, when they are not turning their backs to the camera lens.

These precarious poses, excessive gesturing and movements that seem to be

suddenly executed, communicate a state of emergency, as if they were reflex actions to something that remains unknown to the viewer.

Women's bodies break the repetitive motives of fabrics, curtains, tablecloths and wallpaper as well as the regular geometric patterns of tiles, parquet, wooden slats that envelope the domestic spaces in which the photographs were taken, apparently cosy and homely environments that emphsise even more the strangeness of their behaviour.

Are they practising awkward gymnastic exercises? Are they performing a mysterious choreography designed for a single dancer? Or rehearsing the cryptic scene of a play? Are they sending an encrypted message through body language?

The iconographic source of the series comes to rescue us from drifting through questions and conjectures, providing a buoy on which we can anchor an interpretation of this vocabulary of gestures: the reference to self-defence manuals unveils the foundation of Joanna Piotrowska's work in performance, in this case consisting in the re-enactment of moves taken from those books.

The highly disorienting effect is due to the complete cut-out of the attacker's body, as if to complete the vanishing experiment initiated by Magritte. Self-defence stances — including blocks, strikes, grabs, chokes — are performed against the void, a ghostly sparring partner, a weightless opponent.

The violence is not simply external here either, to echo Magritte's words.

The allusion to an invisible enemy calls into question a more subtle kind of violence when compared to the sensational, physical aggression of men towards women, an oppression so deeply rooted in society that it goes unnoticed.

Before even resisting a man, the unpredictable movements performed by the women, that generate uncertainty in the viewer due to their ambiguity, seem to be turned against the space that surrounds them, arising from the desire to establish a different relationship with it. 'Angel of the domestic hearth', women's space of action has for too long corresponded to that of the house, confined to four walls, which has now become too small. Through reckless poses, the female protagonists of the photographs try to escape a perimeter of constraint that demands ordinary gestures, to appropriate it in an original and unusual way, avoiding the routine mechanism that home and family impose and expect, and refusing to be pigeonholed.

These are small gestures of rebellion against a steady and composed posture, against a balanced composition, against photogenicity, against a neat space that they want to break in order to escape from it.

In this regard, it is worth mentioning Chantal Akerman's cinema which, although not a direct source of inspiration for the series, is a constant reference in Joanna Piotrowska's theoretical research.

In particular *Jeanne Dielman, 23, Quai du Commerce, 1080 Brussels* (1975), a movie that already in its title suggests that the protagonist, a housewife, identifies with her home. The fixed camera documents three days of the young widow's life, regulated like clockwork. Viewers observe Jeanne while she mechanically carries out her usual, banal chores, and unperturbed she prostitutes herself by receiving clients at home, with the same zeal that she puts into housework. Until the perfect choreography of simple daily gestures, performed like a musical score, gets stuck, her daily routine no longer works and a series of small domestic catatrophes leads to the tragic ending.

The 'autistic' body, closed in on itself and its own enigma, which seems to unfold in the photographic series is therefore a misunderstanding. The image is no longer indecipherable if we ideally complete it with, for example, the threatening presence of a man or, better still, if we shift the focus from the body as the subject of the picture to the network of invisible relationships, bonds,

5   Daniel Arasse. *Le Détail. Pour une histoire rapprochée de la peinture*. Flammarion, Paris, 1992.

6   Carol Gilligan. *In a Different Voice. Psychological Theory and Women's Development*. Harvard University Press, Cambridge (MA), 1982, p. 6.

7   Carol Gilligan. *Joining the Resistance*. Polity Press, Cambridge, 2011, pp. 27-8.

8   Georges Didi-Huberman. *Invention of Hysteria. Charcot and the Photographic Iconography of the Salpêtrière*. Translated into English by A. Hartz. MIT Press, 1982, Cambridge (MA), 2003.

hierarchies of power, that an unarmed body, captured in the attempt to wriggle out of constraints, reveals.

That these invisible ties between people represent the core of Joanna Piotrowska's project is made explicit by a group of smaller-sized photographs, also belonging to the series, featuring the encounter between two people — man and woman, mother and daughter — reduced to the contact between their hands, a hand touching a shoulder, or a face. A gap within the narrative, an element of emotional intensification, according to Daniel Arasse's analysis of details in the history of painting, these close-ups of particular gestures invite viewers to a closer perception and communicate on a more intimate level.[5]

The subjects in their entirety are almost completely cut off from this representation. Only their relationship remains visible, distilled in the gestures, tense and suspended as in a magnetic field of energies. At the same time as they vaguely allude to a vocabulary of hand gestures, they deny any possible shared, univocal reading of the relationship they are conveying: a physical and metaphorical arm wrestling between an act of aggression and a magical rite of enchantment.

Carol Gilligan, North American psychologist dear to Joanna Piotrowska, is the author of the seminal book on gender differences, *In a Different Voice* (1982), in which she explores how girls learn to police themselves to conform to social expectations, while introducing an original study on how women approach moral problems differently from men, proving that what some psychologists considered women's deficiencies are rather mere differences from men.

In the female representation of the human condition, characterised by an empathic approach, the world appears to be built on relationships rather than on isolated individuals, and governed by the bonds between men rather than by a system of rules.

Through the observation of several case studies, Gilligan demonstrates 'how accus-tomed we have become to seeing life through men's eyes', that there is no aspect of culture that is innocent of such a sin of one-sidedness; even psychological theorists 'implicitly adopting the male life as the norm they have tried to fashion women out of a masculine cloth.'[6]

(Here, as a memento, the gesture of the woman in Magritte's painting reappears as she tries to shake off the patriarchal heritage.)

In her series, Joanna Piotrowska's voice aligns with that of Gilligan, showing not in a literal, didactic way, but incorporating into the creative mechanism, in the construction of the image itself, the awareness that 'the structures of domination become invisible because they have been internalized. Incorporated into the psyche, they appear not as manifestations of culture but as part of nature — part of us.'[7]

Published in 1982 is also a study by Georges Didi-Huberman, which can be applied to those psychological theorists called into question by Gilligan. In the book *Invention of Hysteria. Charcot and the Photographic Iconography of the Salpêtrière*, the French philosopher and art historian traces the reciprocal relationship between photography and mental illness, describing the practices in use at Salpêtrière, the Parisian psychiatric institution where neurologist Jean-Martin Charcot established the clinical definition of 'hysteria' in the second half of the 19th century.[8]

The origin of the dissertation lies in the disruptive photographs published in the journal *The Photographic Iconography of the Salpêtrière* as documentation of clinical and experimental procedures, including hypnosis, featuring patients in the throes of crises: a visual catalogue of mostly young women immortalised in attacks, screams, and deliriousness, as well as states of ecstasy.

The photographs were taken in the belief that, through the reading of physiognomy, it was possible to obtain a visual lexicon of insanity, but this project proved to be a failure from top to bottom.

9   Ibid. p. 3.
10 Michaela Schäuble. 'Images of Ecstasy
    and Affliction'. *Anthrovision* (Online), 4.2,
    2016, 31 December 2016. DOI: 10.4000/
    anthrovision.2409. Accessed 30 April 2019.
11 Jean-François Lyotard. Op. cit. Note 1,
    pp. 132-3.

After careful analysis of the extreme visibility of the hysterical body, of its excessive exposure, Didi-Huberman came to the conclusion that 'hysteria was a pain that was compelled to be invented, as spectacle and image. It went so far as to invent itself (for this compulsion was its essence) when the talents of hysteria's established fabricators fell into decline. An invention is the *event* of signifiers.'[9] Doctors and hysteric patients came together to stage a scene where hysterical suffering could be fabricated as an art form. 'The clinic and lecture halls in which the patients were "presented" turned into a stage for theatrical performances in which the women enacted the (imitations of) poses and contractures that were perceived as typical for "hysteric" patients at the time.'[10]

Far from being a scientific medical document, the pictures of bodies deformed in impossible contortions rather evoke stale iconographies from witch hunts, Victorian freak shows, and exorcisms, yet another exploitation of women, concealed behind the reasons for medical research.

What other story do these women tell us if we question them directly? Jean-François Lyotard tried it a few years later in his visionary dialogue dedicated to the women of the *Salpêtrière*, coming to affirm that:

The women whose photos we see are not ill, in the process of betraying or exhibiting their symptoms. They are not savages, prey to the trances of divination or exorcism. They are not even actresses caught live at the high-point of their performance. They teach us a sort of theatre of corporeal elements [...] They were photographed to make up an album of hysteria, so as to decipher what they might possibly be saying by these postures. Which implies this: that these bodily states were semantic elements and that they could be linked together by a syntax. One would thus obtain sentences, regulated sequences, and, along with them, meaning. But the photograph which was to make them speak produces an opposite impression on us. It fixes the states in their suspended instability, isolates them one from another, does not restore the syntax linking them. It makes us see tensorial stances. These have a relation to the bodily syntax (of traditional theatre or dance) like that of little elements of sound to composed music. John Cage says that he wants to let sounds be. These photos show what it is to let body-states be.[11]

Between the lines of the long essay by Didi-Huberman, an essential question can be read: how can psychological pain be made visible? By what means, with what language?

The *Untitled* series revolves around something ungraspable, of an inner nature, translated into the visible alphabet of bodies; a psychological essence which paradoxically finds its most spontaneous manifestation in the excess of the body, a body that is unable to adhere to itself.

To this series acts as a counterpoint *Untitled* (2016), a 16 mm film in which a girl, suspended in a black environment, touches some points of her body with her index finger. The constellation she draws turns out to be a chart of the most fragile points of her body, what in self-defence manuals are identified as 'target areas of the body', candidly exposing her vulnerability, staging a defenceless self.

The body keeps on training though: it works out, stretches to regain its own space, greets the sun at dawn, performs muscular awakening.

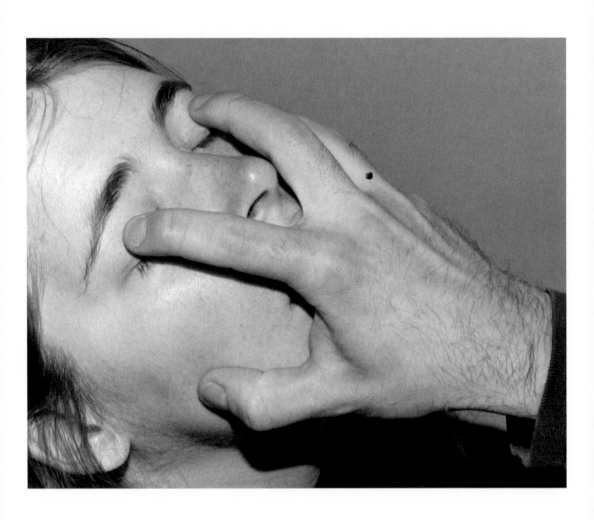

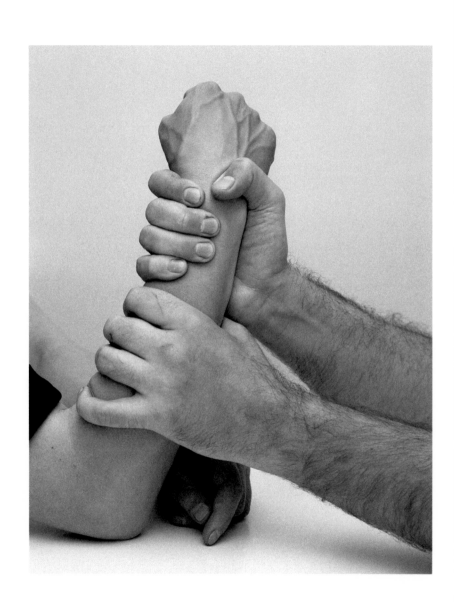

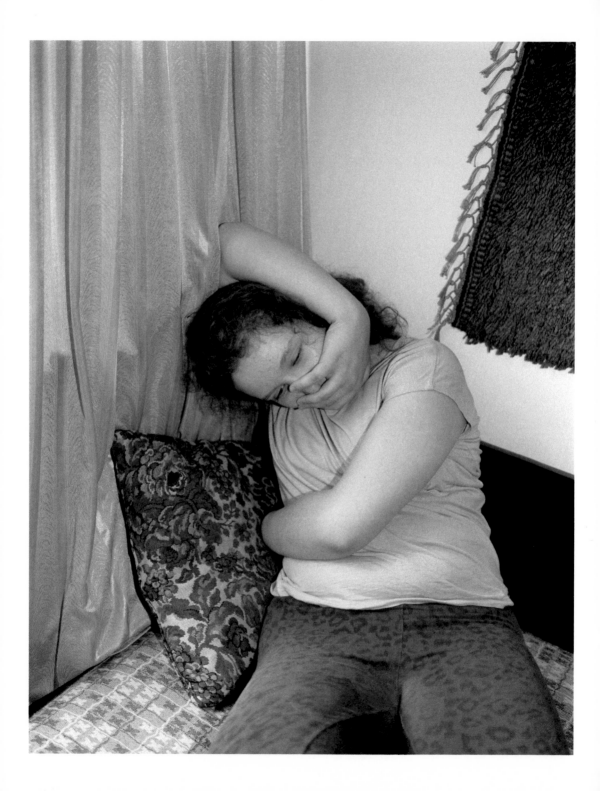

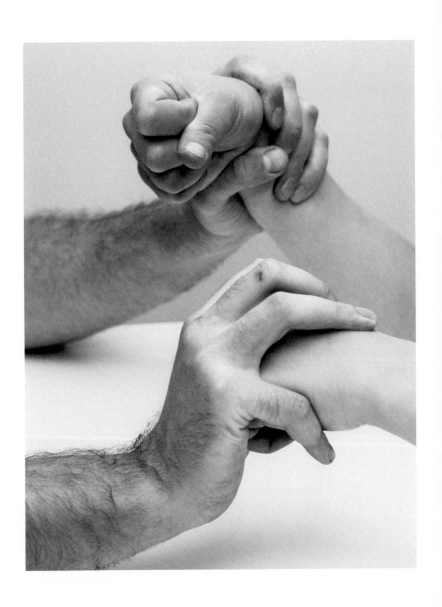

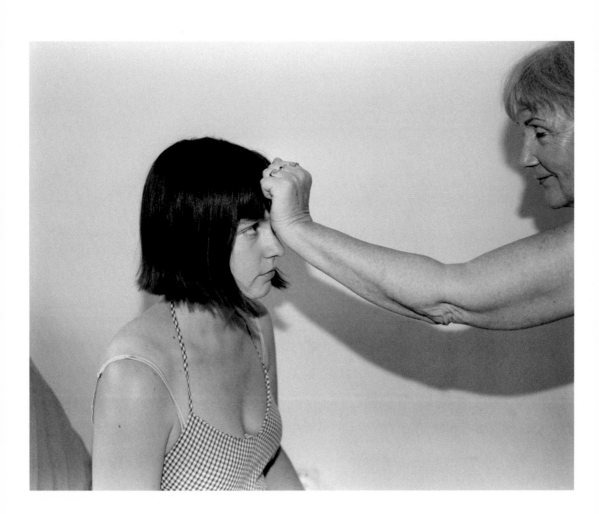

VACANCY
DOROTA MASŁOWSKA

Isolation didn't much hit me with a 'hey there': I'm well-versed in hanging at home. My family discovered lockdown before it was cool. Of course, like a lot of the directives in the homes of our upbringing, this one was as unspoken, and maybe even unnoticed, as it was perfectly clear: it's always better to stay put than to bum around God-knows-where.

I think that that conviction was one of the reasons that grownups thought it was better and more convenient, and if not better, then not much worse, if instead of loitering around preschools I would spend my crucial childhood years at home with my grandmother. There were some other reasons, too, purely pretextual in my opinion, but these days they're hard to debate. It was a different world.

The eighties, an enormous slab of an apartment block and a baby boom. A thousand generations of residents with similar furniture similarly arranged; each morning, mayhem; the wailing of identical enameled teapots, the echo of flushing water, and finally the creak of doors, jangle of keys, the elevator straining and getting stuck between floors, one Fiat or Wartburg after another sputtering to a start and disappearing from the parking lot, taking the grownups to work, the children to preschool and to school.

I remember the awful, thick silence that falls suddenly after everyone has left, that squeals and buzzes among the rooms as if it had been swirling around there all along, unable to die down, particles excited by the morning frenzy.

Then, gradually, it settles, so that around ten or eleven it is completely extinguished,

hardened, having phased into total silence. Did the caregivers who placed me each morning in the sensory deprivation chamber of the empty apartment have no concern for my development? For fostering basic social skills, the ability to tell left from right; familiarity with age-appropriate songs and competence at hiding inedible food in my clothes; and, finally, the heart's first yearnings and the physiological initiations that figure centrally in the recollections of all my peers?

For some reason, in these matters they trusted in my utter self-sufficiency. They thrust me daily into an ocean of vacuity, an ocean of myself, and said: whatever happens, just swim.

So, I'm swimming. Or, rather, I'm just learning not to sink, to float along these empty hours, waiting for the members of my household to come back. I browse the spines of books on their shelves. I rummage through drawers of underwear, study stockings close-up, play cards against myself, watch the farm report on the television, grain being ground down on conveyor belts and the announcement of their prices, I dance to music on cassettes I have found, I try on clothes. I make my own personal documents and stamp them with the seals of countries I've invented, I furnish the fishbowl with plotlines and the rugs with patterns. Independent play is extraordinarily difficult. It's like a language that only one person knows. The loveliest notion easily fades, a madeup world evaporates at the first distraction of its creator. But I somehow get used to it. Boredom

keeps no secrets from me. Not infrequently, it already seems obvious, familiar, secure, even optimal, and the hum of my own brain fluid is its natural soundtrack. At other times, I go stupid and rebel, I try to break out; that's when Grandma reaches for her juggernaut: she tells me that there are wolves outside the door.

In her own childhood, that had been an entirely real threat; I believe her dutifully, though, on the other hand, our tower's stairwell, washed in oil paint the color of diarrhea, doesn't look like their habitat. But in a certain way my grandmother believes it herself. She thinks that life plays out in the home, which an honest person leaves only when necessary (groceries, seeing the doctor). She calls any unjustified departure 'traipsing' or 'bumming around.' Someone who bums around exposes himself to bad weather, to backbiting.

Those are the wolves that have followed her from the village to the city. There may be some war experience in this obsession as well: whoever leaves might just vanish and not come back. Besides, there are other reasons for this natural, voluntary lockdown: there's business to be done in the house, somewhat invisible, but key to its operation. Grandma is bustling.

That's one of those words that I have a visceral feeling for but have to check the dictionary to find out what it really means. 'To devote repeated effort or care.' Grandma's bustling is dozens of imperceptible microefforts, sequences of precise movements squaring away rumpled sheets and scattered pajamas and objects, unfinished tea and breakfast-encrusted dishes. For some reason, I'm not involved in this, I'm not in on it: today, I think that Grandma is jealously guarding the mechanicalness of her ritual, which could be smashed and ruined by a child's jackassery. Move after move efficiently and methodically devotes repeated effort and care, it devotes care repeatedly, putting in effort.

After several quarter hours, the screaming maw of the morning's chaos slowly closes shut. The apartment achieves the status of tidy. This is her daily mandala, an elaborate construction whose result is inevitably destroyed in the afternoon by the returning members of the household. Now, however, the home has been changed for a couple hours into an immaculate museum, where she is the strictest curator and docent.

No running! No taking things out! No jumping! No spilling! No horseplay! Grandma is guarding the effects of the repeated efforts she has performed against chaos's designs. She knows they're ephemeral, delicate, momentary. She wants to enjoy them to the fullest. Today I am perfectly familiar with the feeling when disproportionate exertion succeeds in taming domestic disorder. It is a triumph as great as it is not-great, as delightful as it is irritatingly momentary, fleeting. The wheezing victor looks out over the battle won, knowing that the war is forever lost. And he is seized by a somewhat baleful MAKE THE MOMENT LAST!, a vengeful desire for it to remain. For no one ever to come back here again. For the plates to stay put, the countertops without crumbs, the rugs without dust. In a word, for here no longer to be lived-in.

We struggle like this daily, shoulder to shoulder, with the two mighty struggles of home confinement: Grandma against the infinitude of the mess, me against the infinitude of the boredom. The battle is constant, yet the successes are always momentary, uncertain. Though independent, we cast sly glances at each other, we inspect each other, we observe our twin hopelessness and the repetitiveness of our efforts, and we tease each other with the impossibility of an unambiguous victory. Frequently, we take our frustrations out on each other, falling into

the irritation, mutual distaste, and obnoxiousness typical of those forced onto the same team.

One of my favorite games is building forts out of blankets, seats, and armchairs. What inclines someone to build a room within a room? A home within a home? Walls among walls and a ceiling under a ceiling? Is it some creative horror vacui, an urgent desire to make something that is supposed to organize the emptiness, both physical and meta-physical? Is it perhaps the fear of being consumed? Devoured by home, by its emptiness, silences, routines? Grandma doesn't like this game, because I make a mess. A conflict of interest comes about.

Life smashes, clatters, breaks, wastes, takes things out. Those whose daily antlike labors remain invisible because they consist SOLELY of regularly, arduously, unspectacularly restoring the constantly devastated order have only meaningful sighs, grumbling, and broken arms to defend them — attempts, doomed to fail, to stand guard against the creeping entropy, to hold it back. And vengeful dreaming of a day when no one comes home, tosses their bag on the floor, pulls the blanket from the couch, when no one eats the prepared lunch, setting the dominoes in motion that tomorrow will have to be cleaned up, sorted, put away all over again.

On that day, finally, an eternal, inviolable order will descend, and the cleanest of cleanlinesses, the kind that can never be sullied. This fantasy has no room for dust, cobwebs, and mold, for that illicit life that cohabits with human absence and stillness.

'The web of decay's accompaniment of creativity seems to be a universal structure,' the Polish philosopher Jolanta Brach-Czaina writes in her essay 'Bustle,' which is about the everyday. 'But I believe it necessary to name what is going on here. For the everyday is not only a safe, shallow lagoon of undisturbed boredom, but also the very means by which we live, the site of an insidious, deep-seated, intransigent battle between the forces of existence and of annihilation. […] All of our daily affairs, insipid, apparently meaningless, devoid of weight, are nevertheless what allow us to take part in the ultimate war as it unfolds.'*

* Jolanta Brach-Czaina, *Szczeliny istnienia* (The Fissures of Existence)

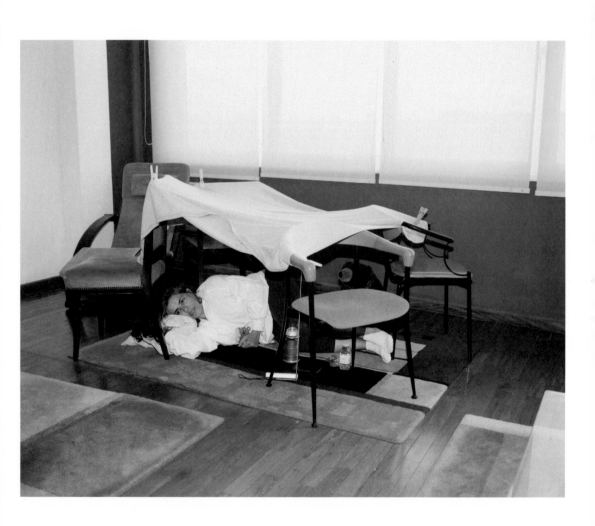

1 TVN24, 'Siedział pod autem i czyhał na
   gołębie. Manul wrócił do zoo zdrowy, ale
   niezadowolony', TVN24, broadcast 14
   October 2020, updated 15 October 2020,
   tvn24.pl/poznan/poznan-manul-uciekl-
   z-zoo-kota-znaleziono-nad-jeziorem-
   maltanskim-4720324. Accessed 11
   December 2020.
2 Jason Hribal. *Fear of the Animal Planet.
   The Hidden History of Animal Resistance*,
   CounterPunch/AK Press 2010, pp. 106-108.
3 Wajeeha Malik, 'Inky's Daring Escape
   Shows How Smart Octopuses Are',
   National Geographic, 14 April 2016,
   www.nationalgeographic.com/news/
   2016/04/160414-inky-octopus-
   escapes-intelligence/. Accessed 11
   December 2020.
4 Ibid., pp. 136-8.
5 Ibid., pp. 151.

ANIMALS BEYOND THE FOREST JOANNA BEDNAREK

Only a few days before I began writing this, a young manul managed to get through the mesh wire of his enclosure in Poznan's New Zoo, in my home city, and escaped. He managed to spend some days at large, most likely hunting pigeons, before being captured and returned to the zoo — 'healthy but displeased'.[1] This is just the most recent case of an animal escaping from this zoo in Poznan: earlier escapees included an elephant, a bear, and several monkeys and apes. Most of them, however, did not get far — typically they were not able to leave the zoo area. The manul — small, well camouflaged and very similar to a domestic cat — was more successful.

Animals have fled or tried to flee from zoos all over the world since this institution first came into existence — and have done so with astonishing frequency.[2] Among the most ingenious of such escapees are apes, who often steal tools with which they open their cages, or who devise ways to disable alarm systems or electrified wires. Octopuses (like the famous Inky[3]) who escape from aquariums also demonstrate their amazing intelligence. Animals imprisoned in laboratories and circuses also try to escape or attack their handlers; orcas working in sea parks — the most famous of which was Tilikum (1981-2017) — also frequently attack their trainers.[4] Although the spokespeople for these institutions often try to present such occurrences as accidents, as merely instinctual reactions on the part of the animals or

as symptoms of individual pathology, in reality they are expressions of intentional agency, of resistance, and thus their source is 'not a psychological disorder', but rather 'a moment of distinct clarity'.[5]

Admittedly, animals cannot write treatises defending their right to freedom. They cannot present arguments for these rights based on the philosophical tradition. For some people, this still constitutes a sufficient basis for denying them the status of subjects, and the freedom from the use and abuse accompanying this status — despite the fact that many humans are also incapable of expressing their rights and defending them with arguments. The institution of human rights, which provides the main discourse and justification for protecting individuals and enables their political participation, is still strongly marked by ideas concerning the subject of these rights, which frame the discourse of human rights and make it possible. These ideas are responsible for the political effectiveness of this discourse, which is evident in the expansion of democratic ideals in modernity, but at the same time they limit its possible applications. This happens because at the time when human rights discourse originated, namely early modernity, scientific accounts of life, evolution and the place of the human being in nature were only emerging. In the 17th and 18th centuries, political theorists still considered reason to be a kind of quasi-metaphysical substance or a faculty that

6   See, for example, John Locke. 'The First Treatise: The False Principles and Foundation of Sir Robert Filmer'. *Two Treatises of Government and A Letter Concerning Toleration*, edited by Ian Shapiro, Yale University Press 2003, pp. 37–8.

7   Ibid. Thomas Hobbes. *Leviathan or the Matter, Forme, & Power of a Commonwealth Ecclesiastical and Civill*, https://www.gutenberg.org/files/3207/3207-h/3207-h.htm. Accessed 11 December 2020. Jean-Jacques Rousseau. *The Social Contract and The First and Second Discourses*, edited by Susan Dunn, Yale University Press, 2002.

8   Jeremy Bentham. *An Introduction to the Principles of Morals and Legislation*. Clarendon Press, 1780, p. 311.

9   Dinesh Wadiwel, 'The War against Animals. Domination, Law and Sovereignty'. *Griffith Law Review*, vol. 18, no. 2, 2014. Dinesh Wadiwel. 'Three Fragments from a Biopolitical History of Animals: Questions of Body, Soul, and the Body Politic in Homer, Plato, and Aristotle', *Journal for Critical Animal Studies*, vol. VI, no. 1, 2008. James Stanescu. 'Beyond Biopolitics: Animal Studies, Factory Farms, and the Advent of Deading Life'. *PhaenEx*, vol. 8, no. 2, 2013. Cary Wolfe. *Before the Law: Humans and Other Animals in a Biopolitical Frame*. University of Chicago Press, 2013.

only humans possess. To be human thus ultimately meant to be something other, something more than simply a living being. Although modernity perceived humans as natural beings, it also viewed them as transcending nature, though this transcendence was no longer grounded in the traditional theological dualism of soul and body, form and matter, spirit and nature. The Enlightenment saw the world as being governed by natural laws, not by God, but this shift was only possible due to Nature being granted the status formerly granted to God. Often this meant assigning God the role of 'the watchmaker' who constructs and sets in motion the clock of the world and then lets it function autonomously, without further interventions (often, this was the first step towards getting rid of God altogether).

Nature, as the creation of God, was a domain of order, both factual and prescriptive. It was an object of scientific investigation and provided a model of ethical behaviour for humans.[6] However, this only seemed to credit Nature with more agency than had been the case in previous eras. Because Nature was considered as an ordered, hierarchical whole, the place that Man occupied in it made him seem distinctive, exceptional. He was both Nature's most complex creation and the only being capable of assuming the role of its caretaker (that is, of having the right to use all living beings for his own purposes). The category of 'Reason' was the principal cause of this distinctiveness — Reason was a faculty that, although natural in its origins, transcended Nature, bringing it to the next level of complexity. This manifested primarily in the human ability to create political communities.

Many modern political thinkers, like Hobbes, Locke or Rousseau, established the legitimacy of the political order on the basis of the state of nature — this fictional condition characterised by conflicts, labour and natural rights, in which the social and the political had their sources.[7] The passage from the state of nature to the political order by way of the social contract was at the same time an overcoming and a preservation of the state of nature. Overcoming, because the social contract allowed the human animal to enter an order of organisation qualitatively different from the one in which all the other animals had to live. Preservation, because the features of the state of nature — like the war of all against all (Hobbes), or the right to the products of our own labour (Locke) — inform the character of the order created by the social contract.

In Man, then, Nature created the only being capable of overcoming Nature and at the same time of realising its fullest potential. As such, only Man can be the subject of natural rights. All other animals are excluded from Reason and from political participation. Although utilitarianism breached this consensus with the proposition that individual welfare be based not on the faculty of Reason, but on the ability to suffer[8], the modern political order is still very much informed by the rights approach (mostly because the utilitarian approach leads to many problematic conclusions). Since they were designed with humans in mind, extending these rights to other animals has come to pose a practical difficulty, despite many scientific discoveries that have confirmed the intelligence and emotional complexity of numerous animal species. As many contemporary theorists state[9], it would require a radical revision of our notions of reason, thinking, subjectivity and communication. However, although radical in its political consequences, it may not ultimately be that complicated — all it takes is a change of perspective, replacing dogmas with attentiveness and sensitivity. If we do this, we will easily notice that animals exercise basic political agency all the time: they escape, attack humans, scream. They express themselves clearly, and it requires

10 Magdalena Komornicka talks to Joanna
    Piotrowska. *Zacheta – National Gal-
    lery of Art*, zacheta.art.pl/en/wystawy/
    joanna-piotrowska-zaduch?setlang=1.
    Accessed 11 December 2020.
11 Michel Foucault. *Discipline and Punish*.
    Translated by Alan Sheridan, Vintage
    Books, 1995.
12 We may argue, of course, that this in
    itself constitutes work: see Jason Hribal.
    'Animals are part of the working class: a
    challenge to labor history'. *Labor History*,
    vol. 44, no. 4, 2003.
13 Martin Heidegger. *The Fundamental Con-
    cepts of Metaphysics: World, Finitude,
    Solitude*. Translated by William McNeill
    and Nicholas Walker, Indiana University
    Press 1995, p. 196.
14 Chris Herzfeld. *Wattana: An Orangutan
    in Paris*. Translated by Oliver Y. Martin,
    Robert D. Martin, University of Chicago
    Press, 2016. Vinciane Despret. *What
    Would Animals Say If We Asked the Right
    Questions?* Translated by Brett Buchanan,
    University of Minnesota Press, 2016, pp.
    1-2. This activity is spontaneous and
    differs from 'animal art' produced by the
    process of mechanical training, which is
    the case, for example, of elephants cre-
    ating figurative paintings (ibid., pp. 3-4).
15 Ibid., pp. 157-8.

colossal stupidity to claim not to be able to understand them.

Escapes from zoos are, then, acts of resistance. But even when the animal is incapable of escaping or seemingly does not display the will to do so, this does not mean that it is content with life in captivity. This leads to the question of zoo enclosures as examples of the 'architecture of oppression'.[10] Just like examples of such architecture built for humans — prisons or factories — they materialise and stabilise power relations. They allow for the exercise of power without resorting to force; they discipline more effectively than orders or violence.[11] The Panopticon, the most famous example of such architecture, materialised power by enabling constant visibility. Zoos perform a similar function, subjecting animals to the human gaze. However, unlike in Bentham's ideal prison, what subjects living beings to power here is not a combination of visibility and forced work, but solely visibility. Animals are being disciplined as objects of spectacle.[12]

The cages photographed by Joanna Piotrowska contain not only places to sleep and eat, but also toys and wooden or rope arrangements aimed at making the spaces more engaging — instruments of 'animal enrichment'. This 'enrichment' is a complicated concept. On the one hand it suggests the idea that the animals imprisoned in such cages are somehow lacking, that their lives are deficient: it evokes Heidegger's definition of the animal as 'poor in world'.[13] On the other hand, it indicates that this poverty is a consequence not of some intrinsic qualities of the animals themselves, but of captivity. The creatures living in these cages, though physically 'safe', are frustrated and bored by the monotony of their surroundings and their daily routine. Enrichment tools thus perform an ambiguous function: they alleviate a condition created by humans and are supposed to eliminate a

lack that is absent in the animals themselves — but in this context they are indispensable. The arrangement of the cages also encompasses numerous quasi-theatrical props — branches with leaves (sometimes artificial), wood, roots arranged into elaborate structures. Unlike the staged scenes represented in other works by Piotrowska, like *Frowst* or *Shelters*, these spaces did not require additional intervention and have a more documentary character — the interiors of the cages are already staged.

Captive animals who, when imprisoned, enter these artificial spaces are capable of amazing feats. Many chimpanzees paint abstract pictures.[14] Wattana the orangutan became famous for her penchant for tying knots: accounts describe her spontaneously creating knotted structures from ropes, twine or wire mesh, which she almost always unknots after finishing. According to Vinciane Despret, in this seemingly purposeless activity we can observe the embryonic form of art and practical mathematical abilities:

> Wattana creates forms. And these forms indicate that the pleasure is not just for play but that they're meaningful, that they express an *act of generating forms*. [...] Of course, she does not prove theorems; she explores the *practical and geometrical* properties of knots *as such*. She recognizes them as the result of *reversible actions,* she has a *functional representation* of them. And she explores them with her body, therefore enacting what they call an 'embodied mathematics'.[15]

Such discoveries not only falsify the idea that we are divided from other animals by some kind of metaphysical chasm, but also lead us to ask questions about the ambiguity of power. Wattana would probably not have developed her abilities in the wild. Her artistic/ scientific practices are a product of oppression, but they also give humans

16 Eva Meijer. *When Animals Speak. Toward an Interspecies Democracy*. New York University Press, 2019, chapter 1. Jennifer Ackerman. *The Genius of Birds*. Penguin Books, 2017. Carl Safina. *Beyond Words. What Animals Think and Feel*. Picador, 2016. Dan Flores. Coyote America. Basic Books, 2017. Irene Pepperberg. Alex & Me. Harper Collins Publishers Inc, 2011. Frans de Waal. *Are We Smart Enough to Know How Smart Animals Are?* W.W. Norton & Company, 2017.

17 Brian Massumi. *What Animals Teach Us about Politics*. Duke University Press, 2014, pp. 7-8.

18 Ibid., p. 12.

a fascinating insight into the talents and capabilities of animals (although we could, arguably, gain this knowledge in other, less oppressive, ways). Numerous studies on different species — apes, corvids, parrots, dolphins, wolves and coyotes, among others[16] — testify to their subjective complexity, proving that earlier findings about, for example, the lack of the 'concept of self' in non-human animals were flawed, due to badly designed experiments or fallacious assumptions. What is more, these discoveries allow us to revise our understanding of the behaviour of other, seemingly less complex species.

Many animals play: we can perceive this activity — earlier downplayed as simply a means to an end (survival), as a way to learn, for example, hunting skills — as the expression of creativity indistinguishable from life itself, as well as a faculty that constitutes the basis for politics.

'In play, the animal elevates itself to the metacommunicational level, where it gains the capacity to mobilize the possible. Its powers of abstraction rise a notch. Its powers of thought are augmented. Its life capacities more fully deploy, if abstractly. Its forces of vitality are intensified accordingly. The ludic gesture is a *vital gesture*.'[17]

Life is creative: it plays, thinks, communicates. Even the so-called 'instinctual' reactions are not as automatic as they may at first seem, because every instinctual reaction is realised, performed, in a different way, depending on the individuality of the animal and the context provided by the environment. Instinct has to be creative, because otherwise it would not react to the challenges posed by the environment:

A normalized gesture is a predictable gesture. If learning were limited to modeling the form of an instinctive act in advance of its instrumental deployment, it would be dangerously maladaptive.[18]

Captive animals express this fundamental ability of life through play. Nonetheless, their play is captured by the disciplinary apparatuses of a zoo, a laboratory or a sea park. It is alienated, subjected to a principle of spectacle for human eyes. However, in Joanna Piotrowska's photographs of the enclosures we do not see their inhabitants. What we see, what imposes on us, are the bars of the cages, which are present in the foreground of all the photographs and are the most distinct of all objects presented. Although we, the viewers, are outside the cages, the bars effectively shape and limit our field of vision. The crampedness of the space is palpable: it is as if we were imprisoned, or at least confronted with the mechanism by which we create structures that imprison both humans and other animals. The cages belong to a continuum of cramped, oppressive spaces, encompassing also domestic interiors: the oppression of non-human animals is in many ways connected to the oppression of humans by humans.

But if the cages are empty, what happened to the animals? Did they escape? Or did they die in these cages, leaving behind the cramped spaces and enrichment tools? The latter possibility seems more real. The photographs evoke an atmosphere of desolation: freedom and play seem far removed from the world they suggest. They are like the documentations of a crime scene, where telling details — like an abandoned basketball or the big knots on the ropes beside the hammock — indicate violent occurrences from the recent past. But what is most important is the fact that the animals are not here; we cannot see them. The animals, if they are present, are beyond the frame. Just like in other works, such as *Frowst* or *Self-Defence*, Piotrowska applies an 'anti-spectacle' strategy — she creates images that make us think about the pervasiveness and ambiguity of power structures instead of showing power in all its violent glory. Images

19 Gary Francione, Anna Charlton. 'The Six
    Principles of the Abolitionist Approach
    to Animal Rights'. *Animal Rights: the
    Abolitionist Approach*. www.abolitioni-
    stapproach.com/about/the-six-princi-
    ples-of-the-abolitionist-approach-to-
    animal-rights/. Accessed 11 December
    2020.
20 Sue Donaldson, Will Kymlicka. *Zoopolis.
    A Political Theory of Animal Rights*. Oxford
    University Press, 2011.
21 Patricia MacCormack. *The Ahuman Man-
    ifesto. Activism for the End of the Anthro-
    pocene*. Bloomsbury, 2020, p. 84.

of suffering, though they appeal forcefully to senses and emotions, might sometimes — precisely because of these features — uphold and perpetuate the spectacle they aim to undermine. Visual representations that make the principles underlying the spectacle visible and undermine them by refusing to reproduce them are, in my opinion, more effective. In this case, the refusal to submit animals to the principle of visibility is more critical than any representation that would graphically depict their suffering.

I have to admit with shame that when I was young and unaware of the issue of animal rights, I liked to visit the Poznan zoo. To be able to see a capybara or an armadillo in person, not on a TV screen, was akin to a religious experience: the sight of a creature that was both very different and mysterious, and yet strangely relatable, was an epiphany. The problem was, of course, that this encounter with otherness was possible due to a system of systemic oppression, and my mystical experience was in all likelihood mostly a projection. As abolitionists state, a necessary prerequisite for pro-animal politics is not some welfarist attempt at improving the conditions of our current use of non-human animals, but the recognition that we have no right to use them in any way.[19]

Animals owe us nothing: just as we have no right to use them as sources of food or experimental subjects, we have no right to treat them as sources of our private epiphanies. Liberating animals does not mean we should cease all interactions with them — on the contrary, it will most likely mean numerous scientific and political interventions aimed at establishing our mutual relations in a non-abusive, egalitarian way.[20] These interventions must be based on a recognition that we are not due recognition, companionship or friendliness from animals — that, as Patricia Mac-Cormack puts it, pro-animal politics will often mean 'bearing witness to the fleeing animal'.[21]

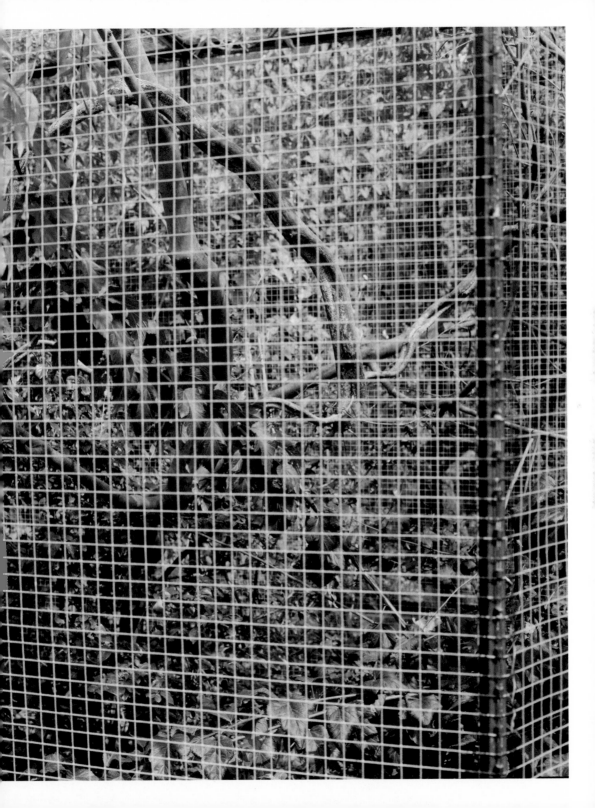

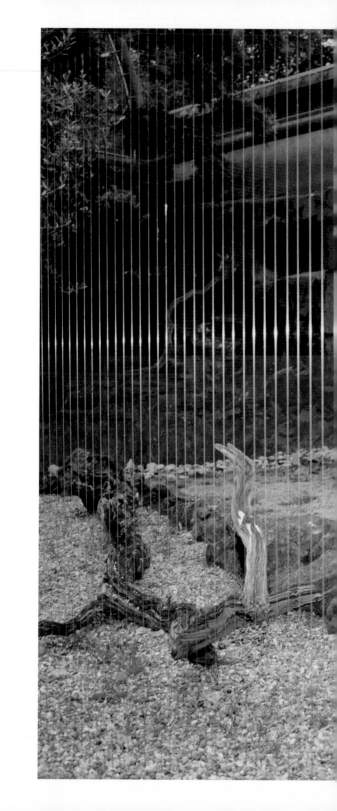

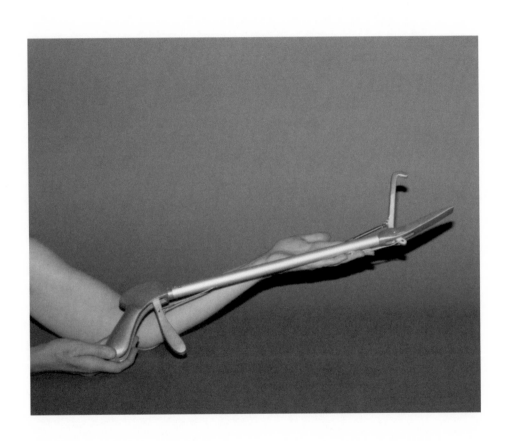

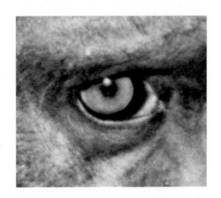

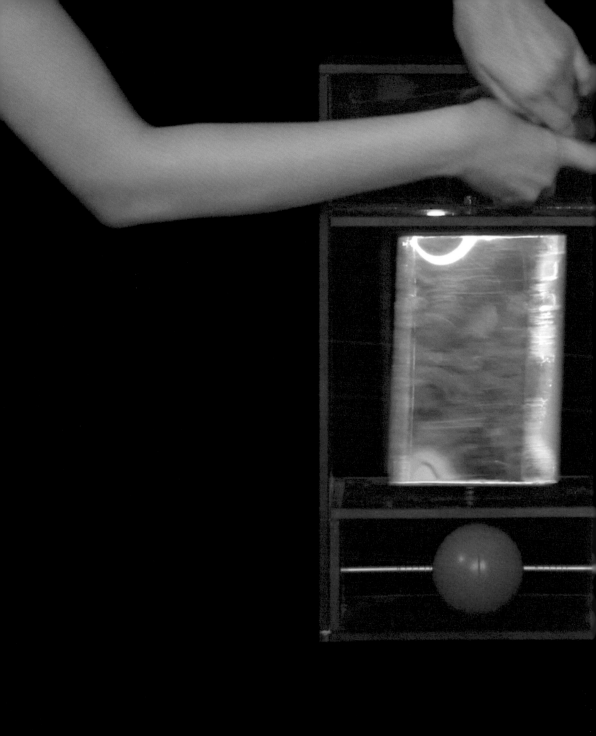

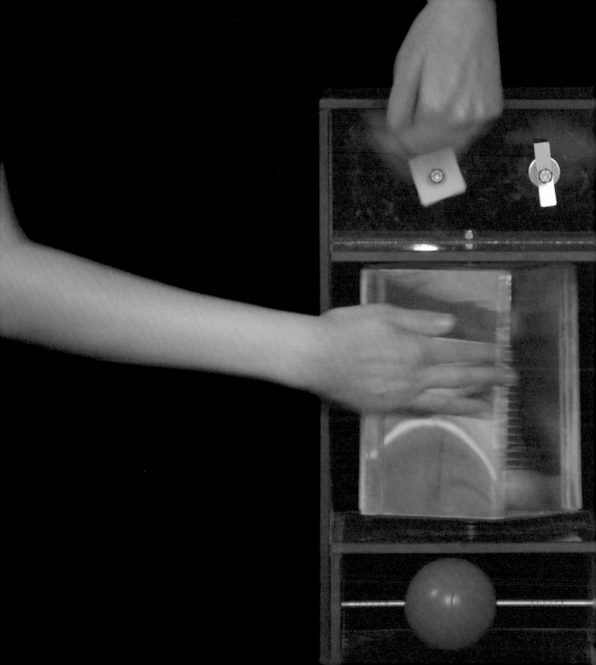

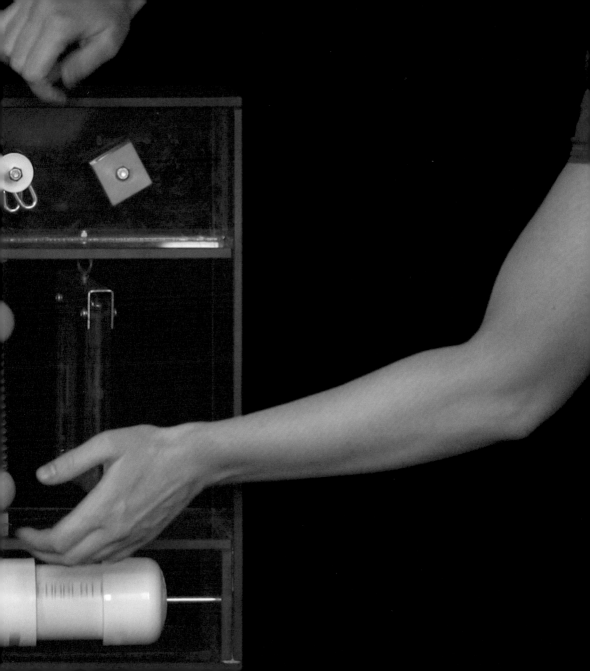

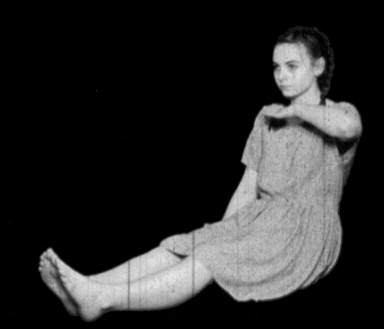

I feel extremely privileged to be surrounded and supported by close friends willing to entertain my best and worst inspirations. Your presence and spirit guide me in my practice.

Brent, thank you for bringing so much laughter and lightness to my life.

Thank you to: my Mum, Bożka, Łukasz, Kaja, Michal Baror, Asia Baś, Veronica, Peslikas, Paweł Olszczyński, Clare Bottomley, Patrick Hough, Magdalena Komornicka, Phillida Reid, Southard Reid, Patrycja, Laura, Thomas Zander, Madragoa, Sara De Chiara, Dawid Radziszewski, Atalanti Martinou, Alex Petalas, Sebastian Edge, Michael Mack, Sofia Karamani, Zuzanna Flaskova, Erich Weiss, Mark McCain, Mirela Baciak, Dominik Czechowski, Juliane Bischoff, Vardit Gross, Diane Dufour, Hammad Nasar, Beatriz Medori, Alicja Czyczel, Morgan Crowcroft-Brown, Elena Filipovic, Arch Athens, Lewis Baltz Research Fund, Artport and Humboldt Books.

Stable Vices
Joanna Piotrowska

First edition published by MACK
© 2021 MACK for this edition
© 2021 Joanna Piotrowska for the images
© 2021 Joanna Bednarek, Sara De Chiara and Dorota
Masłowska for their texts

Pustostan by Dorota Masłowska was originally published
as part of the newspaper *Untitled*, 2020, commissioned
and produced by steirischer herbst '20; project curator:
Mirela Baciak, translator: Benjamin Paloff (Polish-English).
Reprinted here by permission of the author and the com-
missioner.

Little Sunshine, 2019, two channel film projection, 6min
10sec. Film made thanks to Lewis Baltz Research Fund.
Untitled, 2016, 16mm film projection, 03 min. Courtesy of
the artist and Dawid Radziszewski.
Untitled, 2016, 16mm film projection, 02:57 min. Courtesy
of the artist and Dawid Radziszewski.
Untitled, 2016, 16mm film projection, 03:46 min. Courtesy
of the artist and Dawid Radziszewski.

Design by Morgan Crowcroft-Brown and Joanna Piotrowska
Printed in Italy

ISBN 978-1-912339-39-6
mackbooks.co.uk